All verses taken from KJV unless otherwise indicated.

Powers Above, Triangular Powers

by Dr. Marlene Miles

Freshwater Press

ISBN: 978-1-960150-37-0

Paperback Version

Copyright 2023 by Dr. Marlene Miles

All rights reserved. No portion of this book may be copied, photocopied, emailed or held in any type of retrieval system without the express written approval of the Author.

Table of Contents

Introduction 4
Powers Above 7
The Celestial Bodies 10
Triangular Powers 17
The Delay 26
Powers Below 29
The Unbelievers, The Unbelieving 31
Unopposed 35
The Other Side 38
Pastor? 40
Hey, Pray 43
Storm 1.0 45
The One You Have Defied 47
Battlefield Adjacent 51
The Storm 2.0 53
Powers Below – *More Powers* 55
Not a Quick Study 60
For Your Words 63
A War Broke Out 69
Don't Waste It 73
Be That Man 78
Dear Reader: 79
WARFARE PRAYER 80

Christian books by this author 94

Introduction

In my curiosity and search of the powers above, and/or ***Triangular Powers***, I found little, so that is the *why* of this book. We need to learn as much as we can about these things. We want victory. I want victory for you in Christ, and I want victory for myself, also in Christ, Amen.

The ***Triangular Powers*** are three: the sun, the moon, and the stars. They can create powerful and stubborn resistance to your prayers and the answers to your prayers. They can powerfully charge enchantments against you.

You've got to read this book.

Powers Above
Triangular Powers

Freshwater Press, USA

Powers Above

This book will deal with the Powers Above and also discuss the *Powers Below*.

For we wrestle not against flesh and blood, but against principalities and powers, against the rulers of the darkness of this world, against spiritual wickedness in high places.

Ephesians 6

This passage confirms that there are powers above and defines what and who they are and what they do. This book recognizes those powers and spiritual wickedness in high places. This book is primarily about **how those *powers* USE the celestial powers above, that God created**. Those created, celestial powers were created for our good, not for our harm.

God's Kingdom is structured and ordered, and Satan has copied as much of that as he could. Wickedness in high places is defined as follows: ***Powers*** refer to *all* satanic demons. Rulers of the darkness are the oppressive satanic powers of Satan that he uses to control the lives of people. Spiritual wickedness in high places is a more general term indicating the devil's desire to bring demonic possession and have control over all mankind, were it possible.

So, the ***Powers Above*** have learned to interface with the Triangular Powers to bring more oppression and devastation to the Earth and its inhabitants.

- Lord, I pray, let me be among the very elect and that I will not be deceived by the devil, in the Name of Jesus. Amen.

The Celestial Bodies

In Genesis, God created the Heavens and the Earth. He divided the *waters above* from the *waters below*. There is a lot of discussion about whether those waters are literal waters or not, but Genesis describes waters above and waters below. Let's continue and see what the *Spirit* of the Lord is saying.

> God said and let there be a firmament in the midst of the waters, and let it divide the waters from the waters. And God made the firmament, and divided the waters which were under the firmament from the waters

which were above the firmament. And it was so. And God called the firmament heaven, and the evening in the morning were the second day.

(Skipping…)

and God said, let there be lights in the firmament of the heaven, to divide the day from the night, and let them be for signs, and for seasons, and for days and years. And let them be for lights in the firmament of the heaven, to give light upon the earth, and it was so.

And God made two great lights, the greater light to rule the day, and the lesser light to rule the night. And he made the stars also. And God set them in the firmament of the heaven to give light upon the earth. And to rule over the day and over the night, and to divide the light from the darkness. And God Saw that it was good.

We see that God divided the *waters above* from the *waters below*.

God wasn't separating Himself from us. At this time, God was coming down to the Earth in the cool of the day, so God wants to commune with His creation, with man.

God dwells in the Third Heaven and Satan has set up his domain in the second heaven, so was God separating man, who would inhabit the Earth from evil powers in the second heaven? The *powers* spoken of here are in the second heaven and are the evil spirits, principalities and rulers as indicated in Ephesians 6.

They are the same *evil spirits* that the Lord will shake from the heavenlies when Jesus Christ comes at the Judgment. Jesus will come in power and Glory. He will shake everything that can be shaken.

Right now, the second heaven, there are principalities, powers, rulers of wickedness, in high places. These are the fallen angels.

God in Genesis created Heaven and Earth. It didn't say God created the water, but we know God created everything. The water must have been previously created and it was already there because darkness was over the face of the deep. We can surmise that *the deep* was water.

But God said, let there be light. And there was Light three days before God created the sun, the moon, or the stars. God created and all the heavenly ***powers.*** God put a lot of power in these celestial creations. Power is in the sun. Power is in the moon. There is power in the stars, so there are three powerful sources of light that govern the Earth, the sun, the moon and the stars, and these three also can affect human beings, either positively or negatively.

God created the sun to rule the day, the moon is to rule the night, and of course the stars are there as well to indicate to us that it is night.

God made man later in Genesis, and He set man in dominion. We have dominion over the Earth, and over all the works of God's hands. We have dominion over **all** of His handiwork.

God put power into the sun, power into the moon and also into the stars. Then God gave us dominion over all that. That should give us more than a clue of how much power and authority we have, by how much power God has entrusted to us and to our command.

We should be and stay in order to exercise our authority and our power.

> Have you commanded the morning since your days *began,*
> *And* caused the dawn to know its place,
> That it might take hold of the ends of the earth,
> And the wicked be shaken out of it?
>
> Job 38:12-13

We need to command the day We need to command the night, because if we don't, we have learned, and we are learning that evil entities and evil human agents will use God's creation to their benefit and *against* us, especially against Christians.

We need to command the night. We need to command the day in so doing we command these powerful elements of God's creation. Amen.

Recommended book: *Time Is of the Essence*, by this author.

Triangular Powers

Unsaved, unregenerated man has an evil heart, and he has devised a way to use the *power* that's in the sun for other than rooftop tiles to heat a house or heat the water in houses. Evil man has learned to *triangulate* the power of the sun to do evil against other men and the Earth. I'm using the word, *triangulate* since we are discussing the Triangular Powers because evil man is in cahoots with the devil – that's two and then they lasso, the power of celestial bodies to make **three** in agreement to cause their evil to happen in the Earth, and to happen to individuals and people groups. That will be the outcome unless people pray and cancel this evil.

The sun, the moon and the stars, are called the Triangular Powers. This is heavy duty stuff, but we need to know it in order to be victorious in our walk.

In Revelations 12:7 a war broke out in Heaven, and Lucifer was cast out of Heaven. With his tail he brought along a third part of the stars, those were the now fallen angels that came with Lucifer.

Is the war still raging? Even now? Is it raging now? I ask because in the Earth, we are in a war. There is (or should be) a lot of spiritual warfare going on. On the enemy's side, there seems to be quite a bit--, nonstop.

The devil is so committed to warfare against mankind that he would use the strength of the **Triangular Powers** against man.

Can you imagine a supervillain movie where the villain is willing to throw the sun at its victim(s).

Well, it's kind of like that.

On the side of humans, there should be spiritual warfare. But, when there is little, or inappropriate, untimely prayers, the wrong side may win. In this case, when this spiritual war hits the natural, when it hits flesh and blood, there is a lot of devastation.

Something still must be happening in the heavenlies, because the Word says, *Let it be done on Earth as it is in Heaven.*

War broke out in Heaven --, the 3rd Heaven, then on Earth because the entities that started the war in Heaven, fell to the Earth. Obviously, these entities are still angry and warring against mankind. Even the ones that are in high places – above, they still exert influence against man down here.

> For we wrestle not against flesh and blood, but against principalities and powers, against the rulers of the darkness of this world, against spiritual wickedness in high places.
>
> Ephesians 6

Let it be done on Earth as it is in Heaven--, so Earth is supposed to be a mirror image or an image of Heaven or *becoming* an image of Heaven.

That's what we're here for, to have stewardship over the works of God's hands, to subdue the Earth and to make it lovely, to dress the garden, as it were. As we do what we're supposed to be doing--, in our toil and artistic endeavors, there is also warfare.

Warfare is either offensive or defensive or both; it's never neither if you are engaged. The only time it is neither is when there is Peace. Even if you're doing nothing in a war, you could be attacked by the other side that is on the *offensive*. How you plan to do spiritual warfare is between you and God. Do you wait until something happens and come out on the defensive, or do you declare and decree to KEEP the enemy at bay? …Depends on what you know of his tactics and how you conduct your spiritual and prayer life.

When we pray to God and ask Him for any number of things--, things that we need for our life and for godliness. However, sometimes there is a delay in receiving from God. The things that come from Heaven to

Earth have to pass through the heavenlies. Well, there's a second heaven, and that's where Satan lives, that's where his throne is.

What we ask for and need from God is coming from the 3rd Heaven, so it has to go through the 2nd heaven to get down to Earth, to get to us. Our blessings, our answers to prayers, everything that we need, want, and ask for have quite a path to travel, even in the Spirit.

We are reminded from the Book of Daniel how Daniel was waiting for an answer to prayers, but they had to come through that second heaven, and his blessing was held up. It was delayed.

So there's Satan. He's decided to park it in the 2nd heaven, he even put his throne there. He's at the border, the interface between God's

Throne and Earth. He's right there between Paradise and God's people.

So, the only thing between us and Paradise is **the devil.**

Ugh!

The devil is there for a strategic reason, to **obstruct**. He's an obstructionist. He's there to obstruct and interfere with our relationship with God. That obstructionist is also there to interfere with our communication to and from God. Most noticeably to humans is that the devil interferes with blessings and provisions getting to us from God. (Interfering with the Angel(s) that facilitate the answers and provisions we need in the Earth.)

Be reminded from the Book of Job, the devil probably thinks just as he did to Job, if he can mess up all the stuff that we need for life and for godliness, then maybe we will stop worshipping God.

Is that true?

For too many people it might be true, or it has been true. Because not having the things that you need for life and for godliness is a hardship. It can be so dire that it could send a person into survival mode, desperation. Desperation can lead a person into idolatry, which God hates. The Devil knows God hates it when men serve *idols*.

If you go into idolatry--, the devil's got you right then!

The second heavens--, any place and any time the devil can, he makes locations a war zone.

It's a war up there else, why would Jesus be the Captain of the Host of the Army of the

Lord? Why would Heaven need an army? They're not fighting against flesh and blood. This is all spiritual stuff. This is all spiritual warfare. And then why would man be a recruit in the Army of the Lord? Because there is warfare going on all the time, and we are to participate in it.

We will explore this in this book and in the other books of the *Triangular Powers Series:*

- **Powers Above**, Book 1.
- **Sunblock**, Book 2,
- **Do Not Swear By the Moon**, Book 3, and
- **Star Struck**, Book 4.

The Delay

We serve a good God. God is good to us. While we are here on Earth on assignment, God is supplying all of our needs according to His riches in glory. God is not broke. God supplies everything we need, as the Word says, for life and for godliness.

So, you might be asking yourself then, why don't we have those *all things*, all those things we need for life and for godliness? If all the answers to all of our prayers are yes and Amen (2 Corinthians 1:20), where are our ***all things***? Where are the things that we are praying for? What's the holdup?

Well…

We learned from the Book of Daniel, Chapter 10, that once our prayers get through to the heavenlies, then we should see our answers without delay. But we have to get *through* the heavenlies. That's the warfare. That's the delay. **The war zone is the delay.** The war that broke out in Heaven, that is still waging in the heavenlies is the delay.

So we should ask ourselves, what is Heaven going through up there? What are they going through? And since I'm in the Army of the Lord, what's my responsibility regarding that?

Nothing? Are we supposed to just sit around and wait for things to fall from the sky for us? Are we supposed to just sit around and watch TV?

No.

Powers Below

Spiritual warfare is going on in the heavenlies and it's about **_us humans_**. The **_Powers Above_** are waging war against the powers below.

At this point, now that God has created man and given us power and authority, *we* are the Powers Below. Humans of Earth, we are set in Dominion. A person who is set in Dominion has a throne. A person who has a throne, has authority. Authority is power. *We are* the **Powers Below**. The powers above--, the second heavenly stuff are waging war against us.

Since we are in covenant with God, He is fighting battles for us and makes us victorious in war. But we still must do warfare.

The Captain of the Host of the Army of the Lord, God is on our side. He's fighting for us and with us, but we have to also be fighting with Him. Also, the mighty warrior angels of God, are involved in this warfare.

The Unbelievers, The Unbelieving

Pay attention. The people who believe that nothing is going on in the heavenlies, and that this is all a fairy tale, are the ones who won't fight; they won't participate. They won't use their power and their authority, their God-given position and dominion in the Earth to fight and to wage war and win.

Those people will not fight, and then they will also not possess what belongs to their peace and to their Salvation. They will not possess their possessions.

Those people were set in power, they were set in Dominion, just like all of us, so we have to know what's going on in the heavenlies. We have to believe it, and we have to participate in it, doing our part. You must use the power you *have,* or it will be lost. Use it or lose it is the adage.

I'm not talking about people who are misusing and abusing their spiritual power, or people who are appropriating idolatrous power from the devil. I'm not talking about that, *yet*.

I'm talking about **real** Christians, those who *say* they are Christians, and the soon-to-be-Christians who are currently *not believing* and <u>not</u> using their potential God-given authority to help themselves or others to collectively to be victorious in Christian living.

There may be some who are unbelieving now, but in the future, they will use their power that God has given them appropriately. We who are below the Heavens, we should be using our power.

Because people don't believe this is real, sometimes it looks like the enemy is winning. As it is human nature, people like to jump on the winning side and may select evil when they should select God and good, if we Christians are making God look bad, or look like He's not winning.

The devil is the one who is **NOT** winning; he's not, because we've read all the way to the end of The Book, and **we win.**

Even so, Lord Jesus, come.

We've read all the way to the end of the Book, and we know who wins. We win but right now, this can look bad.

Is it because people who are evil want their evil more than the good people want their good? Is it because people who are evil want and pursue after what is evil more than the good people want and pursue after what is good?

Unopposed

**Evil is not stronger than good—
unless it is unopposed.**

We win and we should be winning, and we should be *looking* like we're winning-- all the time. The devil is not stronger than God. The devil has fallen angels that are stronger than he is and sometimes they don't even follow what the devil says to do.

So yeah, there's dissension in his ranks. For real. There's dissension in the ranks of darkness. As prayer warriors, we should exploit that, Amen.

Evil is not stronger than good. The devil is not stronger than God. Hate is not stronger than love. But is it that those who hate, want hate to prevail on the Earth more than those who love, want love to fill the Earth? We must all do our part.

Many times, those who love think that love is a passive, flighty, floaty feeling. All you need is love. Love is the greatest power, and as I said, power must be used. Use it or lose it.

Those who hate, know that hate takes action, so they act on their hate. Christians, all the more, need to act on our love. Because those that are with us, those who love, are more than those who hate.

But if the haters do, if the haters are taking action and those who love are not taking any action, what do you think that's going to look like right now, before Jesus comes?

Yes, I'm calling you to action, saints of God. I'm calling you to prayer and I'm calling you to practice the disciplines of our faith.

We have love, now we can take a nap? Is this why relationships, marriages break up--, assuming it was *love*?

The Other Side

I remind you of the story in the Gospels where the Disciples were crossing to the other side with Jesus--, but Jesus was asleep in the boat. A lot of the Body of Christ right now is asleep in the boat, while there's a massive storm raging.

It's a war.

That war is in the heavenlies, but it affects us on Earth and not just to a small degree, but to a large degree. It's a war.

Christians, where are we?

Asleep in the boat.

There are those who think the pastor is going to handle everything, that's his job, *right*? We pay him for that. We think that the pastor is going to do all the praying and take care of everything.

Show me that model. Moses was over the people who came out of Egypt, it got to be too much for ONE man, so God appointed judges (Deuteronomy 16:18).

One man can't do everything.

Pastor?

Are you kidding me? Aside from that being too much for one man, you'd better ask God for Wisdom and discernment, because a rose is a rose and it smells sweet, but it's got thorns. The Bible warns of hirelings and wolves in sheep's clothing as it describes some so-called pastors. A person could *look like* a pastor, but are they?

Those who look like it and are not could be the reason why a lot of people have run away from churches. They often are the reason why a lot of so-called churches have split up completely.

A person who calls or names *himself* a pastor--, maybe a lot of them, but they're not praying for anybody. They're all about themselves, they are serving themselves.

But let's say you do have a real pastor who is praying for you. Your pastor is not praying *instead* of you. He's praying **for** you, not *instead* of you. You need to see to praying for yourself, yourself. You need to pray about the things that God puts on your heart to pray for. We are called to become Sons of God. See to it yourself.

In addition, praying for yourself, your life and your family's life, the injustices the things that irk you--, that's God showing you what YOU should be praying about and who you should be praying for.

Awake from your slumber. wake up and see to it yourself, PRAY.

Hey, Pray

If you don't know what to pray, ask the Holy Spirit. Pray the Word of God. Pray in the Spirit. Pray. Open your mouth and pray. You'll see why as we go on.

If you think it only takes 5 minutes to pray, then why not take 5 minutes and pray?

If you think praying takes an hour, and there are 500 people in your church. Where in the week will your pastor get 500 hours to pray for each person, or each family? Let's say there's 300 families; where will he get 300 hours in the week to pray for each family?

Is it okay if the pastor prays for 5 minutes for you, or you and your family? You pretty much know that 5 minutes won't cover all the issues you need praying for--, so…you had better see to this yourself. Go ahead and pray.

Storm 1.0

Now, back to that storm on the sea where the Disciples asked Jesus, "*Don't you care if we perish?*"

The people who are dedicated and are praying are wondering of those who don't pray, *Don't you care if we, if* ***all mankind, if the body of Christ, if the purposes of God perish?*** That's why *each* person needs to be doing their part as a Christian. Amen.

The unsaved who will be saved sometime in the future--, thank God for them, they are looking at the Church and maybe wondering, *Why does it look like the devil is winning?*

Seekers and the unsaved are looking at the Church because we are supposed to be an example, and a model to them. They may be thinking without ever moving their mouths, yet are wondering about the saved people who are doing little to no praying, *Don't they care if we perish?*

The One You Have Defied

Woe to those that are at ease in Zion.

Relaxing and living your best life is really not your best life, because we all will have to answer to God for doing *nothing*. If you think having to give account for every idle word is something, how about an idle soul? An idle spirit? An idle mind? An idle prayer life? An idle *life*.

Well...

We should have been doing *something*. We can't act like we don't have a God. You do have a God, don't you? You are saved, right? You talk to God, right?

You don't talk to Him?

You don't talk *about* Him to anybody?

Do you acknowledge God in private *and* in public? You do have a God, right?

David, when coming up against Goliath, said, "*I come to you in the name of the Lord of Hosts, the same one that you have defied.*"

You have a God. You're saved. You are in covenant with God. *Evil* is **defying** your God. **That is the war. Evil is defying our God.** Evil in your life and in the lives of family and people you know, is defying your God, my God, our God. Set in authority, we are the

Powers Below the Heavens, and we should care enough to do something about it.

What are you going to do about it?

Nothing? You believe others are taking care of the problem?

How old are you, now?

Mom and Dad took care of things for you when you were a child.

How old are you, *spiritually*? What things are you capable of doing, spiritually, either independently, or with others? What spiritual things can you do with prayer warriors and other Bible-believing saints of God?

Then you should be doing something about the evil that is coming against the Word, against the will and the plans of God. It's what we are here for.

You're watching TV? Watching football? Enemies of God are raging. What are you doing? If you're in covenant with someone, then their enemies are also your enemies. If you signed up to be in the Army of the Lord, you need to be doing some *army* stuff. What are you doing? Where you *at*?

Yes, God saw what happened spiritually. Yes, God is mighty; God is strong. He is able. But you're assigned to Earth right now. And what you say, your prayer life has so much weight because you're set in Dominion.

Like David, we should have an attitude against those who are defying our God and with those with whom we are in covenant.

Whether we're currently going through something or not, but *especially* if we're going through something right now your attitude should show in your fervent prayer life.

Battlefield Adjacent

Imagine you are the king, you're the leader, you're the president of a country, and you send a troop of soldiers, or a whole army out to war, but they're not doing anything. They're just relaxed over *near* the battlefield. They're not on it, they're just near it, *Battlefield adjacent*. They're just over there oblivious to the fact that there is a battle or a war raging, living their best life. What would you be thinking? Rather, wouldn't you be wondering what *they* must be thinking?

Let's bring it more to the everyday. Let's say you own a company, and you hire staff, small, large, medium, whatever size staff you need. They're not doing their job, but every Friday they're expecting you to pay them--, you know, supply the things that they need for their life, according to your riches that they believe your company has. They want a check every Friday, but they're not doing any work.

Are you kidding me? We ar given power and authority for our purpose , so should we be expecting *anything* from God if we are not doing the assignment that He sent us to Earth to do?

The Storm 2.0

There is hope. Just as when the Disciples were in the boat, Jesus got up and rebuked the wind and calmed the storm, there is hope that the troubles and struggles in your life can be calmed. Even though there are powers above that are raging.

People of God, we can wake up, get up, and we can arise from slumber. We can rebuke the wind with just our words. We can rebuke the storm and we can calm the seas. With just a word, just our prayers, our decrees, and our declarations, we can calm the seas.

Yes, I am saying that sometimes we are in a storm because we haven't PRAYED. Sometimes we are in a storm a long time, or too long because we haven't prayed. You've got your umbrella, rain slick, and you're sloshing about in galoshes, fully equipped to STAY in the storm instead of being prepared to **PRAY** in the storm and PRAY it away. Make it stop.

In authority, just like Jesus you can say, "Peace, be still," and the storm will stop.

Even though there are *powers above*, in our authority and dominion in Christ, and by use of the name of Jesus our God-given power supersedes theirs. But we have to do it correctly, decently and in order.

Powers Below – *More Powers*

In the boat on the raging sea, we can calm the waters *below*-- the powers that are even beneath our feet, beneath the boat. There are powers in the deep, in the oceans and even in the Earth. There's much spiritual evil beneath us, around us trying to oppress us, defeat us or be *in* us.

Jesus cast out a lot of devils. Jesus was training His Disciples. In the Bible, we read that, and we realize He was training us too.

He's teaching our hands to war. Jesus told them, don't marvel that the demons are subject to you, but that your *name* is written in The Book, in the Lamb's Book of Life (Luke 10:20); marvel at that.

I believe, in a sense, Jesus was saying, casting out the Devils may be the least of what you're going to do. But He said, **Greater things you will do because I go to the Father.** Well, what are some of those greater things? Yes, we need demons cast out of people, but Jesus said greater things. I think the greater things are for Earth, for now, not just for the by and by.

Sometimes I think demons are a distraction. Because the real war is in the heavenlies. A war in the Heavenlies is a big problem.

The devil tries to keep mankind busy in our flesh, in one of two ways – enjoying ourselves so much in sin or fighting off oppression that resulted from the sins we enjoyed.

We are tiny people in our flesh, but spiritually, we've got a massive authority. We've got power and authority to speak and assist the angels who are warring against the Resident Evil in high places.

We're doing that, right? Well, good and Amen. If we're not, we need to put on the whole spiritual armor of God, because there's a battle--, there's a war.

If any of us really had any idea of the people, or the numbers of people who don't even know us, but hate us, we might be shocked. They don't know you, but they hate you. They're doing evil in the spirit against you right now--, *just because* they like hate, they like evil, and they're on their evil assignments.

If we really knew and understood, we would all fall on our knees and start praying to God right now.

Proclaiming this among the Gentiles. Prepare war. Wake up the mighty men of war. Joel 3:9

The war that's going on right now, concerns you, your life, your health, your peace. It concerns your business, career, education, your family, your marriage, your bloodline. Your purpose, your destiny, your future, your ministry.

We are all supposed to be able to withstand the wiles of the devil, and that means the devil is tricky, or he wouldn't have *wiles*. Wiles are deceits and sleight of hand. In dealing with the devil most of the time, what it looks like to the natural eye, is **not** even what it is. Most likely, and probably not. It really is not what's going on.

The devil uses smokescreens to mask something else that's *really* happening. But that shouldn't make us hesitate, except to pray and get direction from God, because we should be doing ***greater*** things than even Jesus did.

Not a Quick Study

Yeah, cast out the devils. But what's the other *greater* stuff? Let's ask for spiritual sight, vision and discernment to see past the devil's tricks, wiles and smokescreens and do the *greater* things in the Lord. Amen. We can do it in prayer, in declarations and decrees, with our words. Amen.

For all the people who think you've got the devil figured out? *Really*? Knowing what the devil is doing and what he's going to do is spiritually discerned. You can't just look at a situation with your eyes and decide you know what's going on. The devil is involved, so what you perceive with your flesh is usually **not** what's going on. He uses tricks, deceptions and mirrors.

The devil always puts up an image that's not true. It is one of his *wiles*. So, all of you who think you've got it all figured out? You all know something different than what's in the Bible.

Are you at ease relaxing because you got it figured out?

Woe to those who are at ease in Zion.

The Word says in James 4:7 that to resist the devil, and he will flee from you.

Nowhere in the Bible does it say to ignore the devil, or pretend he's not there, or that he doesn't exist. There's quite a bit of narrative in the Bible about the devil and his multiple names and appearances so we can be aware of his presence or evil hand in the situations that we see in our lives.

For Your Words

One person can put 1000 angels to flight. We each can put 1000 angels to flight. We have command over 1000 angels; I'm just letting that sink in. 1000 people--, that's a lot of people. These are more than flesh people, they are mighty spiritual beings--, powerful mighty angels of God—and <u>*we*</u> can command 1000 of them. 1000 Angels.

These angels, come from the 3rd Heaven, on their way to Earth, but they must go through the war zone of the 2nd heaven.

When we open our mouths and pray, it is serious; we are sending angels from Heaven through a war zone, and the war is against *them*. They won't just be looking at, bypassing the war, or watching reports of it on the news. They will be withheld, withstood, detained, held up, involved, entangled--, with Satan's evil. They've got to get *through* the 2nd heaven, past the seat of Satan, to get to Earth.

The Angels will come for our words, (Daniel 10:12). We have to keep talking, declaring, decreeing, praying. We have to **keep** praying. Keep praying.

Praying once and praying a namby-pamby prayer or your 5-minute prayer--, at least it's something, but a 5-minute prayer will get the angels up from the 3rd Heaven and put them smack in the war zone. We have to pray our angels *through* all the way *through* that war, through that second Heaven past the throne of Satan.

If not, you just put them right in the war zone and what's gonna happen there? They'll be detained, delayed, beat up if possible. It's a war. We have armor and God has weapons. Who do you think is using God's mighty weapons besides us? Angels. There's battling, there is fighting.

If they don't fight and prevail, they may have to retreat, if they can't call for reinforcements--, praise God, they can. But what if they couldn't? In the Book of Daniel, the angel with Daniel's answer was withstood 21 days. The Angel had Daniel's answer right away. That answer was Yes and Amen, just as the Word says. But the angel was withstood. Daniel had to fast and pray. Daniel had to pray that Angel *through--,* in the Name of Jesus.

The Angel doesn't get through, if we give up after only 5 minutes, or we pray without fervor, we just put angels in harm's way, so to speak. We must continue in prayer to pray angels *through*.

If they retreat, Satan will be laughing. This is not funny.

Your prayers won't get answered. Your healing will not come to you. Provisions, education, and successes, education, career, family, marriage, whatever. You are praying to God about your blessings that don't get to Earth because Satan is trying to corrupt your communication, your relationship, your provision and blessings from God to drive you into unbelief, into disappointment, trauma, and idolatry-, straight into Satan's trap.

See how this is not funny? You have 1000 angels at your command. Like Daniel, we use our authority in the Earth to do what we're supposed to do, powering those angels through the heavenlies.

They angels will come; they will come because of your words, because you speak the Word of God. They respond to the voice of the Word of God, and like Daniel, we give them what they need to be successful. We speak those powerful anointed words of God, which God will not return void, but it will perform that where He sends it. Amen.

Then the angels are successful, this blesses you. It blesses the Kingdom. It blesses the lost--, the lost who one day will be saved. And it blesses the whole Earth and the heavenlies because it begins to make the Earth look more like the Word-- ***let it be done on Earth as it is in Heaven.*** It makes the Earth look more like Heaven, the 3rd Heaven.

That's why we put on the armor because it's a war. Until God gives us seasons of rest, it's all whole war every day.

A War Broke Out

A war broke out in Heaven, (Revelations 12: 7), but ultimately, we win. Until we reach the end, we remain in the Earth walking this out.

God is fast. God is so much faster than we are. A day of the Lord is like 1000 years to a man.

War broke out in Heaven, and if that war, for example, was fought for only a day, to

Heaven, that's still 1000 years to us and we're still *walking it out* even though God has been there and completed it already. Flesh is slow, so God has slowed this whole thing down to our speed, the speed of flesh, so we can *get it*, so we can understand it, learn from it, learn to war, learn to win, and keep worshipping Him. It is a test of faith. And a test of patience and other Fruit of the Spirit. But we win.

Because God slowed this down, for us, that is God's **Mercy;** we don't take Grace and Mercy as an opportunity to sin.

Doing nothing is sin. Laziness is sin. Not working is sin. Proverbs says the man who doesn't work should not eat.

Woe to those who are at ease in Zion, because that is sin. To know and do, but do nothing, (James 4:17) is sin.

The war that broke out in Heaven may not have lasted a long time to God, perhaps it was only a day or two--, of course God put an efficient end to this uprising. But *we* are still walking it out.

Recall before Genesis, when man first got here to Earth, the Lamb of God had already been slain. It was already done—*like*, yesterday. God had already done it. Yes, and Amen. He had already answered. The Word says, While you are yet praying, God is already answering. He already knows what we have need of. He is Provident.

So there's the Old Testament and the New Testament, and we're just walking it out. We are still just walking it out. God's waiting for us, and that's Mercy.

You know how impatient you are in your car, for example, if somebody's not taking off as soon as the light turns green. You know how impatient. You are. We all need to work on that.

Before Genesis, Adam and Eve had already sinned. They had already fallen under the Curse of the Law, and they needed to be redeemed.

God had already answered. Thank You, Lord. Thank You, Lord.

So, God is *waiting* for us, waiting for the sons of God to appear, and waiting for the saints to come marching in.

Don't Waste It

So, we don't waste this opportunity, we don't waste the life we've been given. We do something. We do what God says to do. Most often, it's the man who's in bondage to discomfort, disease, and poverty who's really seeking, pressing hard after God, and seeking what God can do for him. God is our rescuer; He's our healer, our deliverer, He's the King of Glory. He's our king. Amen. But those who aren't doing anything have fallen for the *okie doke*. They've been tricked, deceived, they are at risk to be devoured, attacked, overtaken, ripped off, hurt, or worse.

They are not praying because they don't pray. They think that if they don't pray, nothing bad will happen. They may think if they don't pray it won't draw attention to them. They may think that they don't need to pray because that the devil doesn't see them. None of those three statements are true.

When a person is already sold out or in the devil's pocket--, working for the devil--, why would he bother you, other than to ask you for **more sacrifice** for what he (the devil) has already given or promised you?

Anything you get from the devil costs you EVERYTHING.

You are stronger than the enemy. And, if you've got more with you than he has with hiem, and all you have to do is pray, why aren't you praying?

Is it because of unbelief? We can't be ignorant of this. We have to know our position in Christ, our authority in the Lord, and we have to use it. We are set here under Dominion. We have authority, and that's a power.

We are the *powers below* that are supposed to be making the Earth look more like Heaven and not just letting the devil run all over it, and turn it back into chaos when it was dark and void and without form.

The devil likes chaos because he can hide in it.

God likes order. You probably do too.

Perhaps some of the people aren't praying because they prayed already, and nothing happened. You have to keep praying until something happens.

Nobody landed in any mess you may find yourself in, in one day and you shouldn't expect it to be totally cleared up in an hour or in your 5-minute prayer.

Of course, you have to change the lifestyle that got you into trouble. If you are really in trouble and tired of that trouble, you will seek God.

I repeat, most often, it's the man who's in bondage, who has discomfort, disease, illness, poverty, or sickness, who's seeking God, and what God can do for him. He's looking for relief, but ideally, he should be looking for a *relationship* with God. In that relationship relief will come as part of the package.

    Amen.

Be That Man

But the man who is free, the man who is delivered, the man who is well, the man who is whole and has all sufficiency--, that man who is seeking **God**. That man is looking for relationship with God and he is looking for what he can do for God, for other people, for the Kingdom.

Aspire to be that man. Amen.

Dear Reader:

Thank you for reading this book. It was an overview to the ***Triangular Powers***. The other books in this series concentrate each on the sun, the moon and the stars, respectively. They are entitled, **SUNBLOCK, Don't Swear on the Moon**, and **Star Struck**, all by this author.

Now for extended warfare.

WARFARE PRAYER

Arise, mighty warrior, it's time to pray.

Put on the whole armor of God, the armor of light. It's time to assist our angels and their works on behalf of God. On behalf of our Earth, ourselves, and our fellow man.

Lord, arise, and contend with those who contend with me, in Jesus' Name.

Anything in me that's blocking You, Heavenly Father from fighting for me, come out of me right now. Come up and out, in the Name of Jesus. Anything in me that's blocking the heavenlies from fighting for me, Out! Come up and out, in the Name of Jesus. Anything in me that is blocking the heavenlies from fighting for me, come out, come up and out, in the Name of Jesus.

Any wicked power standing to interfere in this prayer, I bind you, in the Name of Jesus.

Any wicked power standing to block this prayer, I bind you, in the Name of Jesus.

Any wicked power standing to intercept my prayers, I bind you, in the Name of Jesus.

I take authority in the Name of Jesus over the effects of the elements, especially the *Triangular Powers*--, the sun, the moon, and the stars, by commanding the day and commanding the night, in the Name of Jesus.

Lord, empower every Angel of God to work on my behalf, and on the behalf of God and all that's good.

I declare the words of the Lord in this prayer. Lord let Your Angels be encouraged, be forceful, be mighty, be victorious, and finish every task to the glory of God. Amen.

I command the Earth to receive heavenly instructions on my behalf.

I command all the elements of creation, and all celestial bodies endowed with power, to take heed and obey.

I command my morning holy in the Name of Jesus and therefore my entire day will be holy. I prophesy the will of God to the morning, so that the first light will shake wickedness from the Earth.

I declare neither the sun, the moon or the stars will smite me today, in the Name of Jesus.

Womb of the morning, incubate good for me all day. Earth, yield your increase unto me, in the Name of Jesus.

I will not be afraid of the evil arrows that fly at noonday, in Jesus' Name.

Any evil using ***Triangular Powers*** to attack me, die, in the Name of Jesus.

Let the evening tide take hold of the ends of the Earth and shake the wicked out of it, in the Name of Jesus.

I command the night, in the Name of Jesus and declare that no evil power, wickedness, ruler or principality, hex, vex, incantation, voodoo, hoodoo, or other black arts, astral projection or other telepathic evil will befall me tonight, in the Name of Jesus.

I declare that no evil desire against me will come to pass, and I forbid all warfare, evil, and corruption from transferring to me, in the Name of Jesus.

I bind and rebuke every creeping *spirit* against me at night, in Jesus' Name.

I bind and rebuke the pestilence that walks in darkness in Jesus' Name. I rest at night because the Lord gives me sleep.

Let your angels guard and protect me, Lord. Give me deliverance in the night season.

I command every demon that threatens my life, back to the dry place, to the abyss where there is no water and no return, in the Name of Jesus. Go! Go into the abyss, from where you cannot return.

Every evil person, entity, or power that is working against my life, my health, my success, marriage, family, Lord Jesus cut off their power from the powers of all the elements and the **Triangular Powers**, in the Name of Jesus.

Lord, break their power and the powers of the waters, seas the oceans, the rivers--, any water, in the Name of Jesus.

Break their power from all powers of the Earth, soil, stones, mountains, trees, rocks, in the Name of Jesus.

Disconnect their power from the network of other *witchcraft spirits,* in the Name of Jesus.

Disconnect their power from the powers of fire, the powers of wind, and the sky, in the Name of Jesus.

Lord, cut off their power from all ***Triangular Powers*** working against me, in the Name of Jesus.

By thunder, by Fire, I break up every altar erected against me, in the Name of Jesus.

Every evil incantation triangulated with the *Triangular Powers*: the sun, Moon, stars, or water, Earth, fire, pot, or charm against me be **canceled** and nullified by the Blood of Jesus.

Every witchcraft kitchen cooking up evil food for me, catch Fire and burn all the way down, in the Name of Jesus.

Lord, cancel every satanic decree against my life, by the power in the Blood of Jesus Christ, in the Name of Jesus.

Every altar against me programmed into the sun, roast to ashes by double Fire and brimstone, right now, in the Name of Jesus.

Every altar against me programmed into the moon, roast to ashes by the Thunder, Fire of God, right now, in the Name of Jesus.

Every altar against me programmed into the stars, be crushed beyond repair by the Thunder Hammer of God, in the Name of Jesus.

Every sleight of hand of the Devil, Lord God, expose it, show me. Let me clearly see what I'm to look at and what I'm to look past, so that I'm effective in life, in prayer, in the Name of Jesus.

Lord, make me among your elite, that I am not deceived by Enemy tricks, in the Name of Jesus.

All tactics, wiles, and tricks of the devil be exposed by the light of the Holy Spirit, in the Name of Jesus.

Fire of God, I call down Fire, Fire, Fire! Fire! against every evil altar erected or working against me or my bloodline, in the Name of Jesus.

Fire, Fire. Fire, I call down Holy Ghost Fire.

Lord God put a hedge of Fire around me, a wall of Fire, a mountain of FIRE, and make me **too hot** for my enemies to even come close to me, in the Name of Jesus.

My life, be charged with the Fire of God that no evil, so hot that no demon can touch, in the Name of Jesus.

Evil Charms demonically charged by **Triangular Powers**, I command you to lose all potency against me, in the Name of Jesus. Return to sender.

Every charm programmed against me, I deprogram you, in Jesus' Name.

Every charm employed against me, I block every access point to me in every dimension, every timeline, age and realm, in the Name of Jesus.

Every charm planned or programmed against me; I cancel your assignment, in the Name of Jesus.

Every charm enchanted against me, Holy Ghost bonfire, burn them to ashes!

Wind of God, blow every roasted charm away like dust, in the Name of Jesus.

Any enchantment of any satanic entity or human agent backfire by fire, in the Name of Jesus.

Any and every satanic animal of any description, flying, crawling, walking, slithering-- charmed against me in any way, I cancel you, in the Name of Jesus.

Arrow of God arise and shoot down any satanic bird flying against me, in the Name of Jesus.

Holy Ghost Boot of God, crush underfoot every satanic ant, spider, or other insect, reptile or varmint sent against me, in the Name of Jesus.

Every charm of my father's house, my mother's house, my friend's house, fake friend's house, unfriendly friends, in-laws, former in-laws, former relationships, exes, evil relatives, co-workers, former co-worker's house, die, in the Name of Jesus.

Lord, reverse every charm programmed against my finances--instead of being a curse let it bless me, in the Name of Jesus.

Every charm programmed against my relationships; the Lord Jesus deny you access to me. Backfire! Return to sender! whatever you have planned for me, let it be unto you, in the Name of Jesus.

Charms against my health, happiness, success, joy, peace, backfire by fire! Return to sender and explode, in the Name of Jesus.

Every power planning to use charms against me, die, in the Name of Jesus.

I disconnect from evil control of **Triangular Powers**, in the Name of Jesus.

Every arrow from the sun, moon, and stars, all **Triangular Powers**, all celestial bodies, release me and locate your owner, in the Name of Jesus.

Triangular Powers go to war **_for_** me, not against me, in the Name of Jesus (X3).

Every evil that has followed my parents, stop following me. I belong to Christ and I'm all in, in the Name of Jesus,

Lord, raise up enemies against my enemies, in the Name of Jesus.

Lord, I release confusion and infighting among my enemies, to total destruction, in the Name of Jesus.

I command the night and the day. I command the sun, moon, and stars, the **_Triangular Powers_** and all celestial bodies, that you will not smite me, or you will work in my favor, for my good, success, blessings, and prosperity in business, life, and relationships, in the Name of Jesus.

For the sake of my bloodline, my destiny, my purpose, my ministry, my family, for the sake of this whole Earth, and for all of the sakes of God, for the sake of the Kingdom, in the Name of Jesus.

Lord, I request 7-fold restoration in all that has been stolen from me by all enemies against me, especially those using Triangular Powers, in the Name of Jesus.

I bind the *spirit of retaliation* and backlash and proclaim that no *spirit*, power, entity, or evil human agent will have opportunity to retaliate against this prayer, in the Name of Jesus.

Thank You, Lord. I count it as done, in the mighty Name of Jesus. **Amen.**

Christian books by this author

AK: Adventures of the Agape Kid

AMONG SOME THIEVES

As My Soul Prospers

Behave

Churchzilla (The Wanna-Be Bride of Christ)

The Coco-So-So Correct Show

Demons Hate Questions

Do Not Orphan Your Seed

Do Not Work for Money

Don't Refuse Me Lord

The FAT Demons

got Money?

Let Me Have a Dollar's Worth (mini book)

Living for the NOW of God

Lord, Help My Debt

Lose My Location

Made Perfect In Love

The Man Safari *(Really, I'm Just Looking)*

Marriage Ed., *Rules of Engagement & Marriage*

The Motherboard: *Key to Soul Prosperity*

My Life As A Slave

Name Your Seed

Plantation Souls

The Poor Attitudes of Money

Power Money: Nine Times the Tithe

The Power of Wealth

Seasons of Grief

Seasons of War

SOULS in Captivity

Soul Prosperity: Your Health & Your Wealth

The *spirit* of Poverty

The Throne of Grace, *Courtroom Prayers*

Triangular Powers – *4 book series*

    Powers Above

    Sun Block

    Do Not Swear By the Moon

    Star Struck

Upgrade Series (3 books)

    Upgrade Your Life

    Toxic Souls

    Legacy

Warfare Prayer Against Poverty

When the Devourer is Rebuked (mini book)

The Wilderness Romance (3 book series)

    The Social Wilderness

    The Sexual Wilderness

    The Spiritual Wilderness

Other Journals & Devotionals by this author:

The Cool of the Day – **Journal** *times spent with God*

got HEALING? Verses for Life

got LOVE? Verses for Life

He Hears Us, Prayer Journal *in 4 different colors*

I Have A Star, **Dream Journal** *in styles for kids, teen,   young adult and up.*

I Have A Star, **Guided Prayer Journal**, 2 styles: Boy or Girl

J'ai une Etoile, Journal des Reves

Let Her Dream, Dream Journal *multiple colors.*

Men Shall Dream, Dream Journal, *(blue, black)*

My Favorite Prayers (in 4 styles)

My Sowing Journal (in three different colors)

Tengo una Estrella, Diario de Sueños

Illustrated children's books by this author:

Big Dog (8-book series)

Do Not Say That to Me

Every Apple

Fluff the Clouds

I Love You All Over the World

Imma Dance

The Jump Rope

Kiss the Sun

The Masked Man

Not During a Pandemic

Push the Wind

Tangled Taffy

What If?

Wiggle, Wiggle; Giggle, Giggle

Worry About Yourself

You Did Not Say Goodbye to Me